The Weights We Carry is the first poe
Seventeen, documenting her solo bike-[
the Scottish highland and Orkney Isl
distance of 658 miles (1058.95 kilometers) and a duration of forty
six days, with mostly wild camping.

C.D. Seventeen is originally from China. She moved to the UK at the age of 17 on her own to study psychology.

She was born in a place called "the south of clouds" (Yunnan province of China), an area with drastic diversity of landscape, religion, culture, music, and arts. "Whoever can speak is a singer, whoever can walk is a dancer" is a famous saying in the country, which describes the artistic Yunnan people. C.D. Seventeen is not an exception. Apart from writing poems, she is also a techno music artist, DJ, and painter.

For more of her work please visit cyberdoll17.com.

The Weights We Carry

Poems from a solo bike-packing journey around the Scottish Highlands and the Orkney Islands

C.D. Seventeen

Published in 2023 by SilverWood Books

SilverWood Books Ltd
14 Small Street, Bristol, BS1 1DE, United Kingdom
www.silverwoodbooks.co.uk

This work depicts actual events in the life of the author as truthfully as
recollection permits. Some dialogue has been retold in a way that accurately
evokes the meaning and feeling of what was said. The story, the experiences,
and the words are the author's alone.

ISBN 978-1-80042-237-7 (paperback)

British Library Cataloguing in Publication Data
A CIP catalogue record for this book is
available from the British Library

Page design and typesetting by SilverWood Books

SilverWood

To all the rebellious souls

CONTENTS

PREFACE

I use poems as containers of my colorful emotions, preserving never-fading memories between the lines. I see verses as musical cords, evoking indescribable feelings. Words are teachers. They never stop asking us thought-provoking questions.

I started writing poems with the purpose of self-redemption. I was brought up in a place where individuality is impossible, freedom is an unimaginable dream, and self-expression is an unforgivable sin. When my world is mostly about competition, productivity, and usefulness, any form of art seems worthless. However, writing poems in a foreign language taught me to be brave to make mistakes and embrace flaws and new possibilities. I learned to let go of the hatred I held towards all the trauma in the past and learn to cure my sense of inferiority caused by the environment I grew up. I learned to appreciate all forms of beauty. And, of course, writing poems created my own freedom.

When freedom is restored, I wish for a rebirth. And this is how my passion for solo long-distance cycling journey started. I wish to know my limits and break them. I want to face my fear and learn what braveness means. I want to unlearn every single word I have been taught, and relearn them in my terms.

This is a poetry collection of my first long-distance solo bike trip in the Scottish Highlands. Twenty-two poems were selected from the draft. Each poem was paired with a photo of the view I saw along the journey when I wrote down the poems. The photos were taken on a half-frame automatic film camera with a kind of film which had a purple-hued character. This, I believe, captures the magical atmosphere of the Scottish Highlands.

The journey started from Inverness and went north from the east coast via Rosemarkie, Tain, Brora, Helmsdale, and John o'Groats. I kept heading north to the Orkney Islands, then back to the mainland to Thurso. After that going back to Inverness from the west coast via Durness, Scourie, Ullapool, Gairloch, and Applecross.

I finished the journey in Burghead on the east coast of Scotland. A trip with a total distance of 658 miles (1058.95 kilometers) with an entire duration of forty-six days, with mostly wild camping.

It was a journey intended to find my true purpose through solitude, but it seemed that what I found was this poetry book.

Join me on this journey of seeking and enjoying the Scottish Highlands and its epic scenery through the lens of poetry.

THE WEIGHTS WE CARRY

I

ELEMENTS OF ANECDOTES

Rootless

Mountain, Mountain,
am I still blessed by you?

The god of my religion,
too far away from my vision.
What type of relation do I have with my possession?
It's the guilt of confession.
It's taboo to show your passion.

I said no
I said no
The most useful word in the human world.
It's the red rejection!

I love you…
But it's just the potion.

Smile, Smile.
The power of loss is to surrender.
Let the word write itself.
It's the practice of a writer.
Control the willingness to be controlled.
Distinguish the 'you' and the YOU.
And,
Freeze…

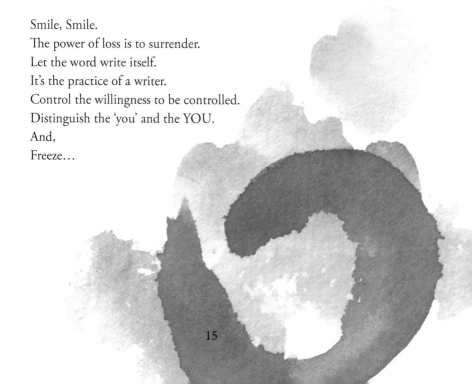

Farewell

The voice of the sea,
the voice of me.
How were dreams born?

Purple coloured fantasies.
I wish you were the one who could read my fear,
so you have the power to curse my atmosphere.

Sorry,
I had to leave you to create my own history,
where you could sing my lines and laugh at my mysteries.

I wish you and I had a living thing,
so what bonded us was not just love but responsibilities.
Since I'm used to feeling that weight with all my senses.

Volition

Sit with a church,
I saw people,
but none of the disciples.
The rotten religion cannot imagine a foreign clergy.

Who still follows the physical existence of a deity?
If so, that's anxiety.

I've got a conflict with my inner narration.
Who picked me to be in this erosion?
I'm just here to be a punk!
Yes!
In front of your kingdom,
and no one ever dreamed to be your queen!

Confession

I would like to feel afloat,
worried to get lost in the dose.
The dose of instant gratification.
The dose of self-deception.

I am the one and only who knows the sea is not blue,
since my eyes cannot see colours as you do.

I wish to live peacefully by the water,
but failed to resist the lure of selling my liver.
It's not the fault of the city.
It's the fault of my own avarice.

Hope

Are you scared of the wind?
Sitting on rocks with white trousers?
There are a million efforts designed for city species
who couldn't conquer the hills but sit for 24 hours.

Real heroes?
Swallowing pain!
Or trained to work in vain?
Kids with no faith won't move their brains,
so get used to burying your cousins for a good name.

But why do we need revolutions?
If there's a house
with hot showers,
near purple flowers.
Just US and sky…

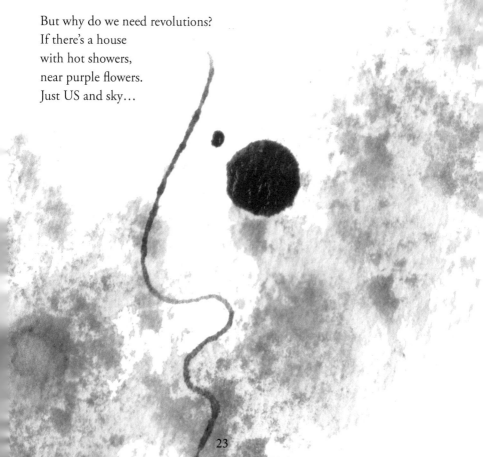

Intentions

I came for dolphins,
instead,
I saw your city wall.
People want to know you as a ruler,
but I wish to know you as a person.
Like a child,
never cared about your wealth,
but about how much candy you can offer to the world.

II

QUESTIONS

I

Would a darker colour scheme pair better with wrinkled skin?
Would silver hair brighten up truths unseen?
Would you choose a wiser mind or older limbs?

II

How much do I deserve to relax?

III

Do I need someone to dive into the dark water?
Not a boy,
nor a dolphin.

III

GRAVITATIONAL PULL

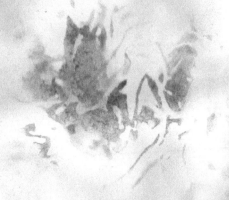

History

Would you hate the one who paid forward your youth?
The root of all your truth.
I got stuck on half of a hill,
stopped by your tomb.

Are you the warlord who owns the key to my wounds?
Or are you just one of us who decorates the tourist's amuse?

Climb or not to climb?
I soar for the downhill bruise.
I wish my nails are painted in red,
like the flowers that symbolize your abuse.
Since I never know your lies,
I can only see you as you describe.

Tyranny

I wish you hear nothing,
don't discard your chance of passive living.
I wish you shut your engine,
don't regret your aim to burn your morning.
I wish you live for crashing,
since there's no end at the end of the road.

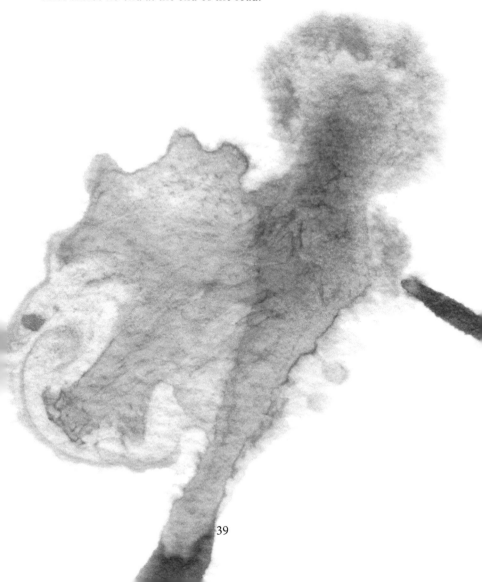

Singularity

Are you a vertical line?
People in pairs are horizontal.
I lost my ability to incline,
forces exerted on me are personal.
Would you show me your mind,
the way you describe your terminal.
What are the differences between you and I?
Gender, mission, height.

Heroism

Why conquer my land?
I defend with my beach sand.
I have flowers for you!
Same colour as what shines.
I knew you would let them dry,
till they matched the colour of your rusted tides.

I'm sorry,
you are trapped in the chaotic time.
Mix mud with your blood for the commander's "must"…

But hey,

I could live for you in a parallel time.
No fire lines,
but colorful rights.
Even the borderlines are still a reason for fights.

Duality

Did I betray myself?
Felt peace in the house of a one-man deity.
Are you the aggregation of idealization?
Or the sinner of shadow elimination?

Evolution

Chop my head off,
for the blessing of the whole tribe.
Crush my personality,
for the circle towards divine guide.
Wait for the thunder to strike for an insight.
Wait for a tragedy to remove a parasite.
How much could I snipe my own pride?
How much of the hypes are forced to be right?

Subjugation

Would you hook your words on a theme
to make it meaningful?
Tag yourself with a meme to make it valuable?
Millions of rocks make a beach noticeable,
but none of the rocks themselves are distinguishable.

Yet,

is it the collectivism scar?
Makes every single thought doubtful,
pick references as navigation stars,
keeping myself looking reasonable.

IV

ACHING IN BLACK

Curses

Do you need a pill?
Hand your power to pure chemistry deal.
Lost your sorrow in surreal.
Learn your values are just sexual appeal.

"What have I done to my nails?"
"I looked like the beauty in the tale!"

You are a mermaid with a tail.
Why would they expect you to dress up in heels?

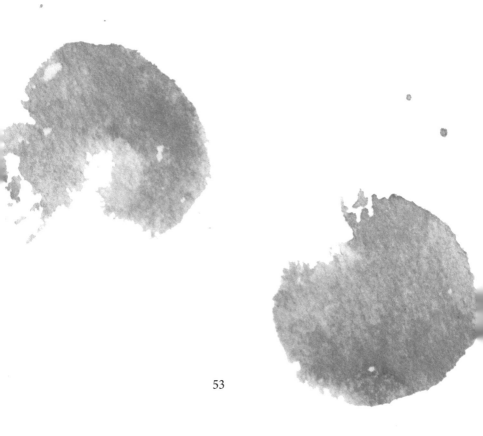

Metamorphosis

I demand your wishes,
pushing stars to burst.
If I owe you answers,
would you choose to learn?
Blindly duplicate furs,
would pigeons speak your verse.
Dig deep till it hurts,
recover or burn.

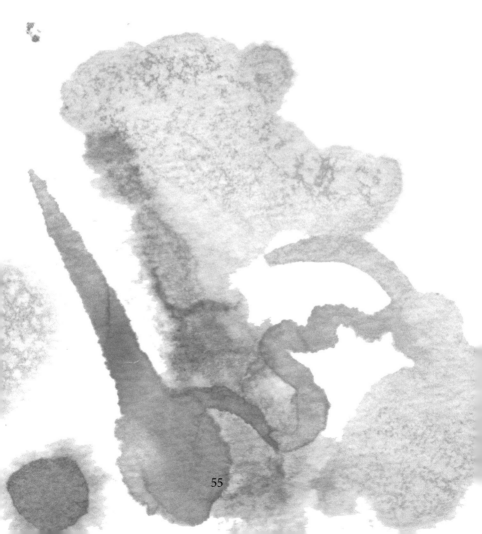

Tragedies

I don't want to get soaked,
afraid of the bike slipping sideways,
cars riding across my broken body.
I don't want to tell jokes,
afraid of words bypassing my cortex,
people knowing my darkened desire.
I don't want to turn it down!
Afraid of missing out on gory years,
waking up to the same dish every single morning.

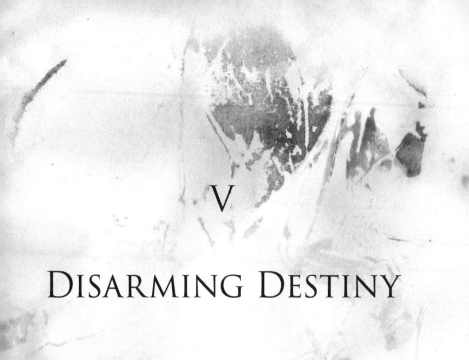

V

DISARMING DESTINY

Redemption

Leave me!
When the ocean stops pouring humid tears.
I swear the cloudy air stirred up some fundamental fears.
Would I disappear into the wind,
undoing my ego identity built up in the urban fairs?
Till I met these boys,
recalling the joy of my teenage years.
Once there was no answer to who I wish to be,
I could sit on the floor instead of chairs.

Unchain

Sing the melody of the northern peaks,
sharpened senses.
How far do I wish to go?
Only BODY knows.
Flood with unknown roads,
goals are just known routes.
I shall keep up with this poisonous crowd,
fatal like this gorgeous doubt.
Who cares if I die proud?
Bury me,
when the wizard's out.

Liberation

Answers, answers, answers!
If I kept riding
will the road straighten itself?
Who left the water empty,
turning every black to blue
I wonder at the inverted world.
Filling blanks in vow,
will I ever end this journey?
Forget me all,
into the wild.

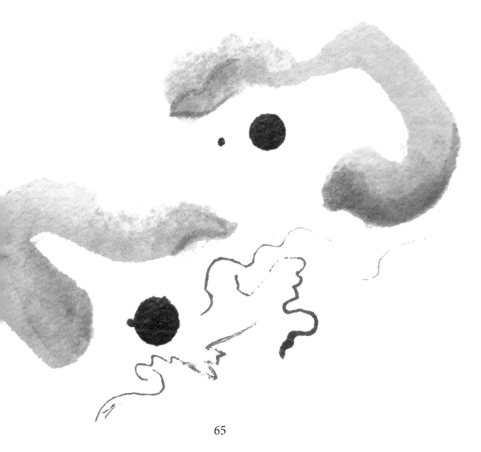

Ingram Content Group UK Ltd.
Milton Keynes UK
UKHW050646070323
418149UK00004B/172